Poems
for
Writing 2

Poems for Writing 2

Sheila M. Lane
Marion Kemp

Blackie

Blackie & Son Limited
Bishopbriggs, Glasgow G64 2NZ
450 Edgware Road, London W2 1EG

© Sheila M. Lane and Marion Kemp 1976
First published 1976

ISBN 0 216 90172 3

Printed in Great Britain by
Robert MacLehose & Co. Ltd
Printers to the University of Glasgow

Preface

Poems for Writing are intended to supplement **Towards Creative Writing** so that the whole form a series. Book 1 is for Lower Juniors, and Book 2 for Upper Juniors or Middle Years.

Each book consists of twenty themes in double spreads. Within each theme there are poems and photographs which provide stimuli for children to write their own poems. The aim has been to collect material which is of intrinsic merit, so that the literary quality will contribute to the children's own reservoir of language. The photographs are used in such a way that horizons should be broadened and fresh ideas formed in the children's minds.

In **Book 1** extensive use of the "model" poem is made. Ideas are deliberately sown so that children can "write their own poem" with confidence. It is believed that, "when poems are used as starting points for original work—they are intended to provide a stimulus, to stir up the dormant imaginative processes. . . . Imitation is the natural way to maturity and self-dependence." (James Reeves)

In **Book 2** more emphasis has been placed on the collecting of ideas and language, so that the children have:

a material of literary merit before them,

b a reservoir of language to which they have contributed,

c an opportunity to extend their thinking before writing their own poems.

Acknowledgments

The authors and publishers make grateful acknowledgment to the following for permission to use copyright material.

Poetry

C. A. Reitzels Forlag for "The Kayak Paddler's Joy at the Weather" trans. by William Thalbitzer from *The Ammassolik Eskimo : Contributions to the Ethnology of the East Greenland Natives*, Part 11, No. 3: Language and Folklore (Copenhagen, Meddelser om Grønland, vol. XL, 1923).

Penguin Books Ltd. for five *tanka* from "Poems of Solitary Delight" by Tachibana Akemi and "Returning to His Old Home" by Otomo Tabito from *The Penguin Book of Japanese Verse* ed. and trans. by Geoffrey Bownas and Anthony Thwaite, © 1964; fourteen lines from "The Door" by Miroslav Holub from *Selected Poems* trans. by Ian Miller and George Theiner, © 1967, and the Polynesian rain song from *Maori Tales* (Take Part Series).

Geoffrey Summerfield for a slightly shortened version of "Windy Boy in a Windswept Tree".

E. M. Greene for "I Saw the Wind Today" by Padraic Colum.

André Deutsch for "I Saw Two Pigs" by John Cunliffe from *Riddles and Rhymes and Rigmaroles*.

Macmillan, London and Basingstoke, for the extract from poem thirteen trans. by Kevin Crossley-Holland from *Storm and Other Old English Riddles*.

The University of California Press for "The Snail's Monologue" by Christian Morgenstern from *Christian Morgenstern's Galgenlieder* trans. by Max Knight, copyright © 1963 by Max Knight.

Laurence Pollinger Limited for "Heavy Words" and "Light Words" by Alastair Reid from *Ounce, Dice, Twice* published by Dent.

Rand McNally & Co. for "Halloween" by Marie Lawson from Child Life Magazine, October 1936, copyright 1936, 1964 by Rand McNally & Co.

Gerald Duckworth and Co. Ltd. for the extract from "Overheard on a Saltmarsh" by Harold Monro from *Collected Poems* ed. by Alida Monro.

Oxford University Press for the extracts from the Authorized Version of *The Old Testament*.

Victor Gollancz Limited for the extract from "The Mirror of Perfection" from *God of a Hundred Names* compiled by Barbara Green and Victor Gollancz, © 1962 by Victor Gollancz Limited.

John Murray (Publishers) Ltd. for "Karakia" from *Maori Myths and Tribal Legends* by Antony Alpers.

R. C. Scriven and B.B.C. Publications Ltd. for the extract from *The Seasons of the Blind*.

Photographs

Barnaby's Picture Library pages 9, 13, 15, 39 and 47.

Pace pages 11, 29, 33 and 43.

Will Green pages 17 and 21.

S.P.A.D.E.M. for "The Blue Owl" and "Woman Weeping" by Picasso, © by S.P.A.D.E.M., Paris, 1976, pages 19 and 31.

The Tate Gallery Publications Dept. for "Structure 14C" by Stephen Gilbert, page 23.

The Minerva Press Limited for "Uncle Lubin" by W. Heath Robinson, page 25.

Popperfoto page 27.

Antony Penrose for "Woman Weeping" by Picasso, page 31.

Henry Grant page 35.

Josip Generalic for his painting "Fish on Flowers", page 37.

The Trustees of the British Museum page 41.

The John Hillelson Agency Ltd. page 45.

Contents

Song of joy

This is a traditional Eskimo poem translated into English.

The Kayak Paddler's Joy at the Weather

When I'm out of the house in the open, I feel joy.
When I get out on the sea on hap-hazard, I feel joy.
If it is really fine weather, I feel joy.
If the sky really clears nicely, I feel joy.
May it continue thus for the good of my sealing!
May it continue thus for the good of my hunting!
May it continue thus for the good of my singing-match!
May it continue thus for the good of my drum-song!

How many times does the Eskimo poet end a line with the phrase
I feel joy?

How many times does a line begin with the phrase *May it continue
thus . . . . . ?*

Make a collection of phrases which you could say to show that you
feel filled with happiness.

I feel glad	I'm filled with elation

Make a collection of phrases which show that you want your feelings
of pleasure to go on for a long time.

Let it last like this	May it so remain

Is the child in the photograph happy to be on the beach because of:

> *the feel of sand beneath her feet,*
> *the smell of the sea,*
> *the taste of the salty fresh air on her lips,*
> *the sound of the waves on the shore,*
> *the sight of the gulls circling overhead?*

What kind of weather do **you** most enjoy when you are at the seaside?

Do you enjoy:
> *paddling and swimming,*
> *going out in a boat,*
> *fishing for . . . . . ,*
> *playing or making . . . . . ?*

Write your own *Song of Joy*.
Use your own word collection to help you.

Feelings of pleasure

These poems are translated from the Japanese.

Poems of Solitary Delight

What a delight it is
When everyone admits
It's a very difficult book,
And I understand it
With no trouble at all.

What a delight it is
When, skimming through the pages
Of a book, I discover
A man written of there
Who is just like me.

What a delight it is
When, spreading paper,
I take my brush
And find my hand
Better than I thought.

What a delight it is
When a guest you cannot stand
Arrives, then says to you,
'I'm afraid I can't stay long,'
And soon goes home.

What a delight it is
When, of a morning,
I get up and go out
To find in full bloom a flower
That yesterday was not there.

Tachibana Akemi

The boy in the photograph isn't solitary. He looks delighted to be receiving the admiration of all the other children.

What physical activities do you enjoy? Do you feel happy when swimming, running, cycling or playing games?

Do you have feelings of happiness when you are on your way to visit a special place or a favourite person?

What gives you a feeling of quiet satisfaction?

Do you sometimes feel thankful when something is over?

Perhaps you sometimes feel:

> *What a delight it is*
> *When . . . . .*

Write your own *Poems of Solitary Delights*.

Feelings of fear

Have you ever felt real fear?

Windy Boy in a Windswept Tree

The branch swayed, swerved,
Swept and whipped, up,
Down, right to left,
Then leapt to the right again,
As if to hurl him down
To smash to smithereens
On the knife-edged grass
Or smother
In the close-knit quilts of moss.
Out on a crazy limb
He screwed his eyes tight shut,
To keep out the dizzy ground.
Sweat greased his palms;
Fear pricked his forehead.
The twisted branches lunged and lurched,
His body curved, twisted, he arched
His legs and gripped the bark
Between his ankles.
Then the mad-cap, capering wind
Dropped.
The branch steadied,
Paused,
Rested.
He slowly clambered, slowly, back,
Slowly so safely,
Then dropped
Like a wet blanket
To the rock-like, reassuring ground.
Finally, without a sound,
He walked carefully
Home.

Geoffrey Summerfield

The Royal Navy helicopter is just completing a real rescue.

How might you feel if you were attached to a rescue-line and your body was swaying in the air?

What movements might your body make on the swinging line?

Make a collection of words and phrases which you could use to express your feelings of:

a **Fear**

I stared in terror at . . .   Sweat greased my palms

b **Relief from fear**

I breathed steadily now   The fear ran from my . . .

Write a poem about being *Rescued*.
Use your word collections to help you.

Open your eyes

What is outside **your** door?

The Door

Go and open the door.
Maybe outside there's
a tree, or a wood,
a garden,
or a magic city.

Go and open the door.
Maybe a dog's rummaging.
Maybe you'll see a face,
or an eye,
or the picture
    of a picture.

Go and open the door.
If there's a fog
it will clear.

     Miroslav Holub

Begin your own poem by writing about something which is **really** outside your door at home:

  When I open the door,
  I see . . . . .

As you look at the same scene, open your eyes a little wider than usual. Discover some tiny details which you didn't notice the first time:

  When I open my eyes wider,
  I see . . . . .

Now open the door of your imagination. Look around in a hopeful way. What else would you like to see?

  Through the door of my imagination,
  I see . . . . .

In the foreground of the photograph you can see the clear shapes of cow parsley flowers and stalks growing in the hedgerow. Try to distinguish other summer plants.

As you look farther across the field you can see the blurred silhouettes of a variety of trees in leaf. What might they be?

Imagine what lies beyond the mist on the horizon. What may become visible when the sun has broken through the haze?

Write a poem about the picture.

You could make an anthology of your own poems called, *When I Open My Eyes*, illustrated with pictures from magazines.

Reflections

As you read this poem open the door of your imagination.

I Saw the Wind Today

I saw the wind today :
I saw it in the pane
Of glass upon the wall :
A moving thing,—'twas like
No bird with widening wing,
No mouse that runs along
The meal bag under the beam.

I think it like a horse,
All black, with frightening mane,
That springs out of the earth,
And tramples on his way.
I saw it in the glass,
The shaking of a mane :
A horse that no one rides.

Padraic Colum

When the poet looked in a pane of glass, he imagined that he could see an image of the wind in the form of a horse.

Shining surfaces can send back true images which are called reflections.

Think of surfaces which could give you **reflections** :

A glass mirror on . . . . .
The polished wood of . . . . .
A sheet of . . . . .
A metal . . . . .
A wet . . . . .
The waters of . . . . .

You have probably guessed that this picture is upside down.

Stare at the strange house in the upper part of the photograph.
The eerie effect is created by the ripples of water on the surface of
the river.

Pretend that you are standing and gazing into the water.
Does the house look like *a moving thing*?

Does the movement of the water make it tremble, quiver, shake, or
appear to vibrate?

Does it look like an underwater dwelling or . . . . . ?

Is it a house in which no one lives or . . . . . ?

What could lie beneath the shapes and forms which blur the clear
outlines of the picture?

Write your own poem about the picture.

Possible or impossible

This is a puzzle poem.

I Saw Two Pigs

I saw two pigs bake a pie,
I saw a girl spread wings and fly,
I saw a swan beating a drum,
I saw a man the size of my thumb,
I saw a nut go to the moon,
I saw a space-ship as big as a spoon,
I saw a fork that told a tale,
I saw a book as big as a whale,
I saw a ship upon the sea,
And all these things you too may see.

John Cunliffe

Poems like this are called **punctuation puzzles**.

You can make sense of it by:

a taking away the comma after the word at the end of each line, then
b putting a dash after the noun in the middle of each line.

Try reading *I Saw Two Pigs* again, like this:

I saw two pigs——bake a pie
I saw a girl——spread wings and fly
I saw a swan——beating a drum
I saw a man——.....

Which shapes are easy to identify in this unusual picture?
Can you see shapes representing an owl, a tree, thorns, a window,
moonlight, a man or a woman?

The picture can **start you off** with your own punctuation puzzle,
e.g.   *I saw the moonlight——sitting on a tree*
           I saw an . . . . .——swim out to sea
           I saw . . . . .

Here are some rhyming phrases which could help you:
           fly round and round   *eating ears of wheat*
           crawling along the ground   *with shoes upon its feet*

Your puzzle could end like this:
           I saw a ship upon the sea,
           And all these things you too may see.

Riddle poems

This is an Old English riddle.

Four stiff-standers,
Four lily-landers,
Two lookers,
Two crookers,
And a wig-wag.
                    Traditional

Could two lookers be two eyes?
Could two crookers be two horns?
Four stiff-standers could be . . . . .
Four lily-landers could be . . . . .
A wig-wag must be . . . . .

Think about how animals **use** different parts of their bodies.

Look at your own body.
Think of unusual ways to describe how some of your body parts can
be made to work.

Make a collection called:

Naming of Parts

For a tail: *a swisher, a twirler, a mophead, a* . . . . .
For a nose: *a twitcher, a sniffer, a* . . . . . *, a* . . . . .
For teeth: *rows of* . . . . . , ... ,
For . . . . . :

Make word chains to describe **parts of the owl**:

Eyes: (staring)(glowing)( )( ) **gogglers**

Beak: (hooked)( )( ) **tearer**

Wings: (folded)( )( ) **flappers**

Claws: ( )( )( ) **grabbers**

Write your own riddle poem about a bird

Guess the answer to Neil's riddle:

> *Four, groovy trotters,*
> *One, stubby sniffer,*
> *Two, perky listeners,*
> *A belly of a life!*
> *With two sleepy blinkers*
> *And a curly-whirly.*

Make your own *Book of Riddles*.

An Anglo-Saxon riddle

This Old English riddle was discovered in the manuscript of **The Exeter Book** and was translated by Kevin Crossley-Holland from the Anglo-Saxon, in which it was originally written.

> *I saw a strange contraption, an experienced traveller,*
> *grind against the gravel and move away screaming.*
> *This strange creature could not see; it had no shoulders,*
> *arms, or hands; on one foot this oddity*
> *journeys most rapidly, far over*
> *the rolling sea. It has many ribs,*
> *and a mouth in its middle, most useful to men.*
> *It carries food in plenty. . . .*
> *Tell me if you can,*
> *O man of wise words, what this creature is?*

Notice:
a how the riddler gives clues without naming the object of the riddle,
b how the riddler compares the Anglo-Saxon ship with the body of a human being,
c how the riddler makes his listener smile with these comparisons.

Write down all the words in the riddle which can be used to describe a human being in some way, even though the riddler may admit that a ship doesn't have them.

Write a chain of words which mean **strange**:

(remarkable) ( ) ( ) ( )

The artist who created this polished aluminium shape just called it **Structure 14C**.

Write some phrases which could begin a riddle about **Structure 14C** and which would make a listener think and wonder about an un-named object.

e.g. *Before me stands a structure of strange form,*
I see this most extraordinary shape.

Use one of your phrases to begin your riddle.

When you study **Structure 14C** very closely, does it make **you** think of a bird, insect, aeroplane, dancer, ... ?

Decide on **your object for comparison**.

Go on writing your riddle, saying what is the same and what is different. How does your object move? What does it do?

You could end your riddle by flattering your listener. The Anglo-Saxon riddler said:

Tell me if you can,
O man of wise words . . . . .

Limericks

Limericks are comic, five-lined verses.

There was an Old Man of Dumbree
Who taught little owls to drink tea,
For he said, "To eat mice
Is not proper or nice,"
That amiable Man of Dumbree.

Edward Lear

Notice:
a how the five lines are arranged by the poet,
b the shape of the limerick: **two** longer lines,
                                    two shorter lines,
                                    one longer line.

To write a limerick you need two pairs of rhyming words.
e.g.   Dumbree   mice
                        and
            tea   nice

This limerick is in **The Blue Peter Book of Limericks**, all made up by children between the ages of 5 and 13.

There was a young hamster named Nelly,
Whose whiskers were sticky and smelly,
This was not, if you please,
Some strange new disease,
But a 'strordinary liking for jelly.

Maureen Lacy

Could you complete either of these two lines as a beginning for your own limerick?

> *There was an old man called . . . . .*
> *Who went for a ride to the moon.*
>
> *There was an old lady called . . . . .*
> *Who said, "This is making me dizzy,"*

It's a good idea to use the **name** of a person to rhyme with line two, after you have thought this second line out.

Your limerick could continue:

> *I think I shall land*
> *Down there on the sand,*
> *Or you'll soon see the end of poor . . . . .*

The last line (line 5) of a limerick usually uses the same rhyming word as line 1. Many limericks end with the idea:

> *So that was the end of . . . . .*

A monologue

Guess the name of the creature talking.

Shall I dwell in my shell?
Shall I not dwell in my shell?
Dwell in my shell?
Rather not dwell?
Shall I not dwell,
shall I dwell,
dwell in shell,
shall I shell,
shallIshellIshallIshellIshall . . .?
Christian Morgenstern

When the snail has to decide whether to stay in its shell, or come out, it becomes very confused.
Do you think that it becomes so entangled with its thoughts that it goes to sleep?

Could you make a bird talk to itself so that it gets sleepier and sleepier?

You could begin by making the bird say:

Need I rest in my nest?
Need I not rest in my nest?
Rest in . . . . .

Write: *The Bird's Monologue*

Ask yourself this question:

> *Do I dare to stare at a bear in its lair?*

Answer your question by saying:

> *I don't dare to stare.*

Make up: *A monologue when staring at a bear*

Write some more monologues, using different word patterns.
Begin by having a **clear thought** in your head.

e.g.   For a hippopotamus:

> *Will I wallow in water?*

Then make your hippopotamus decide whether it will wallow in
water or whether it will **not** wallow in water.

Make a collection of *Tangled Thoughts*.

Words at work

The sounds of the words in these poems help to suggest the meanings.

Heavy Words

(to be used in gloom or bad weather)

DUFFLE
BLUNDERBUSS
GALOSHES
BOWL
BEFUDDLED
MUGWUMP
PUMPKIN
CRUMB
BLOB
   Alastair Reid

Light Words

(to be said in windy or singing moods)

ARIEL
WILLOW
SPINNAKER
WHIRR
LISSOM
SIBILANT
PETTICOAT
NIMBLE
NIB

Alastair Reid

Did you notice that the **heavy** words all had letters O or U in them?

Did you notice that the **light** words all had the letter I in them?

When you write your own **words at work,** you could make up **new** words.

Does the expression on the boy's face suggest:

Happy Words

(to be said when all seems right with the world)

MELODIOUS

CONCORDIOUS

. . . . .

Miserable Words

(to be said when the world seems upside-down)

DOLEFUL

DOOMY

. . . . .

Angry Words

(to be said when in a bad temper)

FURIOUS

FUMATIOUS

. . . . .

Make a collection of *Words at Work* poems.
Don't forget that you can make up **new** words.

Making images

Read this conversation aloud, in two parts, with a friend.

Halloween

"Granny, I saw a witch go by,
I saw two, I saw three!
I heard their skirts go swish, swish, swish—"

> *"Child, 'twas leaves against the sky,*
> *And the autumn wind in the tree."*

"Granny, broomsticks they bestrode,
Their hats were black as tar,
And buckles twinkled on their shoes—"

> *"You saw but shadows on the road,*
> *The sparkle of a star."*

"Granny?"

> *"Well?"*

"Don't you believe—?"

> *"What?"*

"What I've seen?
Don't you know it's Halloween?"

Marie Lawson

Do you always see what is really there, or do you have the ability to form images in your mind?

Granny is **not** imaginative and she explains that:
the black witch's clothing is made by the shadows on the road,
their twinkling shoe-buckles are sparkling stars,
the swishing sound of their skirts is being made by the autumn wind in the tree.

This imaginative picture by Picasso, shows the artist's creative ability.

Can you guess what Picasso was seeing, hearing and thinking when he was painting this famous picture?

How might Picasso have answered these questions:

> *Picasso, what is your woman wearing?*
> *Picasso, what is your woman hearing?*
> *Picasso, what is your woman thinking?*
> *Picasso, why is your woman crying?*

Make the questions, with your own imaginative answers, into a poem.

You could call it: *The Artist Answers*

Treasured possession

Have you ever overheard a conversation which was not intended for your ears?

Overheard on a Saltmarsh

Nymph, nymph, what are your beads?

Green glass goblin. Why do you stare at them?

Give them me.

     No.

Give them me. Give them me.

        No.

Then I will howl all night in the reeds,
Lie in the mud and howl for them.

Goblin, why do you love them so?

They are better than stars or water,
Better than voices of winds that sing,
Better than any man's fair daughter,
Your green glass beads on a silver ring.

Hush, I stole them out of the moon.

Give me your beads, I desire them.

        No.

I will howl in a deep lagoon
For your green glass beads, I love them so.
Give them me. Give them.

     No.

Harold Monro

The boy's face shows that he values his treasure, but the girl's face and hands show that she wants to own it too.

What do you think the treasure is?

What could the girl be saying to the boy? Do you think that she is trying to persuade him to give up his **possession** by arguing:

> in a pleading, begging way,
> by coaxing and flattering,
> by making continuous demands,
> by promising an exchange of possessions,
> by using threats?

Who has the last word?

You could write a poem about *A Treasured Possession*.
Will you be the one who possesses or the one who covets the treasure?

Persuading people

This is a short extract from a long poem in which two children imagine that they are looking in on a scene which is not intended for their eyes.

Goblin Market

Come buy our orchard fruits,
Come buy, come buy :
Apples and quinces,
Lemons and oranges,
Plump unpecked cherries,
Melons and raspberries,
Wild free-born cranberries,
Crab-apples, dewberries,
Pine-apples, blackberries,
Apricots, strawberries ;
Come buy, come buy ;
Taste them and try.

Christina Rossetti

Would it be easy to persuade people to buy produce if the seller's market cry were: *Come buy, come buy ;*
Taste them and try?

Make two lists, one for fruits ending with -s in the plural and one for fruits ending with -ies.

e.g.

-s	-ies
peaches	gooseberries
apples	strawberries
. . . . .	. . . . .

As you make your list, think of words to describe the colour, freshness, texture and taste of the fruits.

e.g.   sweet, downy peaches   plump, juicy gooseberries
         sharp, crisp, red apples   morning-picked strawberries
         . . . .

The owner of this market stall has a variety of fruits and vegetables to sell.

Traders often change the names of some of their wares slightly so that they are easier to, "call".

A flower seller might cry: *Posies of roses,*
Gillies, Sweet-willies . . . . .

Some names can be shortened:
e.g.   tomatoes can be called as **tommies**,
       cauliflowers can be called as **collies**,
       mushrooms can be called as **mushies**.

Make up *Market Calls* which would persuade people to buy
different kinds of produce from: a **fish** market,
                   an **antique** market,
                   a **china** market,
          or   . . . . .

In praise of the Creation

We can read about the Creation in the Bible.

Genesis

*In the beginning God created the heaven
and the earth. . . .*

*. . . And the Spirit
of God moved upon the face of the waters.
And God said, Let there be light :
and there was light.
And God saw the light, that it was
good. . . .
And God said, Let the earth bring
forth grass, and the herb yielding
seed, and the fruit tree yielding
fruit after his kind, whose seed is
in itself, upon the earth. . . .
And God saw that it was good.*

Do you think that the Psalmist was inspired and guided by **Genesis**
when he wrote:

*. . . O Lord my God, thou art very great ;
Thou art clothed with honour and majesty.
Who laid the foundations of the earth. . . .
Thou coveredst it with the deep as with a garment. . . .
Thou causeth the grass to grow for the cattle,
And herb for the service of man :
That he may bring forth food out of the earth ;
The trees are full of sap. . . .*

Psalm 104

Do you think that the artist who painted **Fish on Flowers** could have been inspired by these verses from **Psalm 104**?

> *. . . The earth is full of thy riches.*
> *So is the great and wide sea, wherein are things creeping innumerable,*
> *both small and great beasts.*
> *There go the ships : there is that leviathan,**
> *whom thou hast made to play therein.*
> *a huge sea-monster

Make images in your mind of tropical birds, chameleon-like lizards and desert and Arctic mammals all emerging into a newly created universe.

Write: *A Psalm of Creation*

You could use phrases from **Genesis** or **Psalm 104** to help you.

> e.g. *O Lord my God, thou art very great . . . . .*
> *The earth is full of they riches . . . . .*
> *And God saw that it was good . . . . .*

In praise of the Elements

Ancient peoples believed that fire, air, earth and water were the foundation of all things.

Franciscan Prayer

Be Thou praised my Lord, with all Thy creatures
above all Brother Sun,
who gives the day and lightens us therewith.

Be Thou praised, my Lord, of Sister Moon and the stars,
in the heaven hast Thou formed them, clear and precious
and comely. . . .

Be Thou praised, my Lord, of Sister Water,
which is much useful and humble and precious and pure.

Be Thou praised, my Lord, of Brother Fire,
by which Thou hast lightened the night,
and he is beautiful and joyful and robust and strong.

Be Thou praised, my Lord, of our Sister Mother Earth,
which sustains and hath us in rule,
and produces divers fruits with coloured flowers and herbs . . .

Praise ye and bless my Lord, and give Him thanks,
and serve Him with great humility.

Think about the importance of water to all living things.
The poet describes Sister Water as, *much useful and humble and precious and pure.*
Make a collection of words and phrases to describe **Sister Water**:

life-giving   cleansing

The sight of **nimbus** (rain clouds) in the sky must bring feelings of great joy and also relief to people who have suffered from drought and dust-laden winds for many months.

In some parts of the world **rain-making rituals** are performed. People make up incantations which are said or sung to encourage rain to fall:

> *The small rain,*
> *The long rain,*
> *The lasting rain,*
> *Rain! Rain!*
> *Oh, Rain God,*
> *Water our Earth.*
> Polynesian Rain Song

Write your own *Rain Song* and then make up a Hymn of Thanksgiving: *In Praise of Receiving Rain*

Spells and incantations

The Maori people of New Zealand say that their North Island was pulled up from the depths of the ocean by Maui, using his magic fishing hook. As he hauled in his line, he chanted a magic incantation called a:

Karakia

Blow gently, Whakarua, *Wind of the North East
blow gently, Mawake, *Wind of the South East
my line let it pull straight,
my line let it pull strong . . .
The land is gained,
the land is in the hand,
the land long waited for . . .
O Tonganui,
why do you hold so stubbornly there below?
The power of Maui's jaw bone is at work on you,
you are coming,
you are caught now,
you are coming up,
appear, appear . . .

Tonganui was the great God of the South of the Sea who lived on the ocean bed.
Muri was Maui's grandmother.

Many words and phrases must have gone through Maui's mind as he pulled and strained on his fishing line.

Write some phrases to continue the Karakia after:

    a My line let it pull strong,
     . . . . .
    b The land long waited for,
     . . . . .
    c Appear, appear,
     . . . . .

Make these phrases into a new **Karakia of your own**.

This photograph of a Sorcerer's carved staff comes from Sumatra.
Maui carved his magic fish hook from his grandmother's jaw bone.
Do you think that the decorations on the head of the staff are made
of birds' feathers and human hair?
What could the wooden carvings represent?

Imagine yourself as the maker and owner of a sorcerer's staff.
What would you use your staff for?
How could different parts of your staff help your enchantments?
Would you call on magical spirits or elements?
What are your thoughts as your enchantments show signs of
working?
How do you feel when your magic **has** worked?

Write: *My Sorcerer's Spell*

Pleasures and delights

Do you share this poet's pleasures?

These I Have Loved

These I have loved:
        White plates and cups, clean gleaming,
Ringed with blue lines; and feathery, faery dust;
Wet roofs, beneath the lamp-light; the strong crusts
Of friendly bread; and many-tasting food;
Rainbows; and the blue bitter smoke of wood;
And radiant raindrops couching in cool flowers;
And flowers themselves, that sway through sunny hours,
Dreaming of moths that drink them under the moon;
. . . . furs to touch;
The comfortable smell of friendly fingers,
Hair's fragrance, and the musty reek that lingers
About dead leaves and last year's ferns . . .
And oaks; and brown horse-chestnuts, glossy new;
And new-peeled sticks; and shining pools on grass;—
All these have been my loves.

Rupert Brooke

The poet uses four of his five senses when he describes some of the familiar, everyday things which give him great pleasure.
Which sense does he **not** use in this extract?

Make a collection of **sounds** which you like to hear.
Think of sounds which bring immediate pleasure to your ear:
e.g.   birds singing,
            the voice of someone you love.

Think of sounds which you connect, in some way, with **other**
things: e.g.   The sizzling sound of your favourite food cooking.

Walt Whitman, the American poet wrote:

> ... *The apple-buds cluster together on the apple-branches* ...

In his poem, *Grass of Spring*, Whitman writes about how Nature awakes from the long sleep of winter.

> ... *The grass of spring covers the prairies,*
> *The bean bursts noiselessly through the mould in the garden,*
> *The delicate spear of the onion pierces upward* ...
> ... *The young of poultry break through the hatch'd eggs,*
> *The new born of animals appear.* ...

Write your own poem about those things which give you pleasure and delight.
You could call it: *These Things I Love*

Memories

Have you ever "moved house"? The English poet remembers happy days in his childhood home.

I Remember

I remember, I remember
The house where I was born
The little window where the sun
Came peeping in at morn;
He never came a wink too soon
Nor brought too long a day;
But now, I often wish the night
Had borne my breath away.

Thomas Hood

When the Japanese poet returns to his empty house he is overcome with sad memories.

Returning to His Old Home

The empty house
With no one there
Is harder even
Than when I journeyed,
Grass for my pillow.

With my wife,
Together we made it—
Our garden with its streams.
Now the trees grow tall and rank.

My wife planted
This plum-tree.
When I look on it
My heart chokes,
And the tears well up.

Otomo Tabito

Wild flowers growing in the blackened ruins are the only signs of life in the empty and abandoned street.

Why did all the families who once lived in tidy houses, with small neat gardens, move away?

Where have they gone?

Why has the old man returned?

What has he found? Has his "find", awakened sad or happy memories?
What will he do with his, "find"?

What will he say to himself on his way back to his present home?

Write a poem about someone who returns to a house where he or she once lived and finds that it has been abandoned.

Varieties

These four lines are the beginning of a poem of praise for the variety of pattern and colour in Nature.

Pied Beauty

Glory be to God for dappled things—
For skies of couple-colour as a brinded cow;
For rose-moles all in stipple upon trout that swim;
Fresh-firecoal chestnut-falls; finches' wings. . . .

Gerard Manley Hopkins

Read this word chain:

(patterns)(marks)(patches)(spots)(streaks)(stripes)

Make a word chain of the words used by the poet to describe different marks and touches of colour:

(pied)(d . . . . .)( )( )

The poet uses *finches' wings* as an example of design and colour patterns in birds. Make your own collection of other examples:

      e.g.   a thrush's throat,
               a bee's yellow and black body.

Make **poetic phrases** by using a descriptive word with each of your examples and changing the pattern of your words:

      e.g.   the speckled throat of thrush,
               the banded yellow-black of bee.

Add new ideas:

      e.g.   dapples of sunlight.